nobody's boy

Cataloging-in-Publication data is on file with the Library of Congress.

ISBN 1-883982-58-8

Distributed by University of Missouri Press

Cover design by Creativille, Inc.

Printed and bound by Sheridan Books

nobody's boy

JENNIFER FLEISCHNER

Missouri Historical Society Press
St. Louis
distributed by University of Missouri Press

Contents

Foreword

My official career is that of historian and museum professional, but a valid description of my work in both these fields is that of a storyteller. The stories I tell are often other people's, sometimes the stories of men, women, and children who, like George in this book, lived a long time ago. History can be considered a story that we pass down through generations.

We don't know, and are not likely to find out, whether George had a friend named William or what a slave boy's conversations were like. But we do know for a fact that George and his mother, Elizabeth Keckly, lived in St. Louis and were owned by a man named Hugh Garland. We have a historical record of this. We also have an idea about what slavery in St. Louis was like, and we know that enslaved people took great risks to get their freedom. *Nobody's Boy*, a fictional tale but based in the author's thorough research, tells some of that historical fact.

As a historian in charge of a public museum, it is my job to bring history into the present so that we can look at our past and decide how to make a better future. As young members of your community, you should learn about—and from—those people who were here before you. This book is a means of seeing through someone else's eyes and looking at a world long gone but still a part of us.

—ROBERT R. ARCHIBALD, PH.D.
PRESIDENT, MISSOURI HISTORICAL SOCIETY

Family Tree

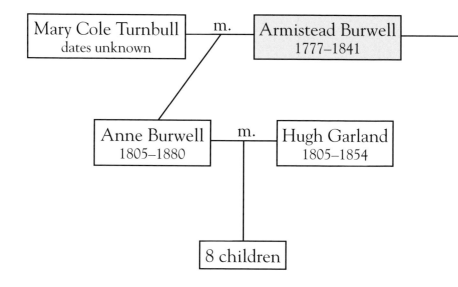

Mary Cole Turnbull
dates unknown

m.

Armistead Burwell
1777–1841

Anne Burwell
1805–1880

m.

Hugh Garland
1805–1854

8 children

of George Kirkland

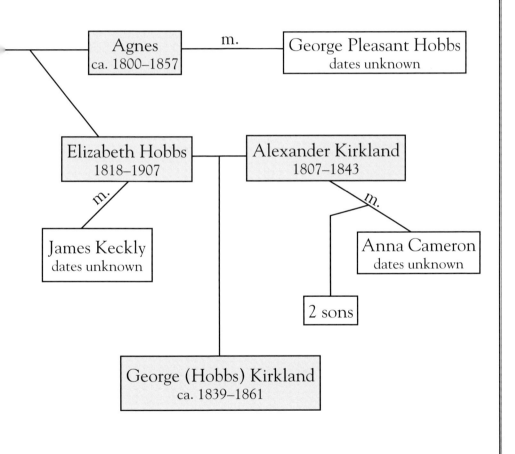

Agnes
ca. 1800–1857

m.

George Pleasant Hobbs
dates unknown

Elizabeth Hobbs
1818–1907

Alexander Kirkland
1807–1843

m.

m.

James Keckly
dates unknown

Anna Cameron
dates unknown

2 sons

George (Hobbs) Kirkland
ca. 1839–1861

Garland's George

To the white folks he was Garland's George, because he was Mr. Hugh Garland's slave, and that's how a slave was called. To his mother, Lizzy, who had named him after her slave father—not her real father, but her slave mother's husband—he was Georgie, Georgie Hobbs. Her real father was her master, a Virginian named Armistead Burwell. She talked about him about as much as she talked about the white slaveholder who fathered George. That is, she never spoke of either man.

But George had heard his father's name—Alexander Kirkland—from the other slaves. He knew his mother was ashamed of this man. He sometimes felt she was ashamed of him.

"George! George! Get on out here!" Mr. Garland's voice interrupted his thoughts. "Hurry up! What's keeping you?" George already stood in front of his master, Mr. Garland, by the time he finished yelling for him. The afternoon light cut through the library window on a sharp slant, so that George had to squint to see Mr. Garland's pale, thin face. "Take these papers over to Mr. Norris," Mr. Garland said, thrusting a bundle in George's general direction. Lyman D. Norris was Mr. Garland's law partner. George noticed how his master's hand shook and decided to ask his mother about this later. "He'll give you a letter in return. Be quick, now." They were working on a big case involving a slave named Dred Scott, who was suing his mistress for his freedom. George had heard it discussed among the Garland slaves.

George couldn't wait to be out the door. He hated household chores—waiting on the family table, sweeping the floors, hauling wood for the fires—but he loved being sent on any errand, no matter what it was. He loved walking through the St. Louis streets, looking into shops, nobody minding him for a change. He could feel downright invisible out there, on his own, and it was a wonderful feeling. There were so many free black people in St. Louis in 1853, that no one, unless they knew him, could tell he was a slave. In fact, George's skin was so light and his hair so smooth, it was hard to tell he wasn't white. George used to hate being so much lighter than his mother and the other slaves. But as he'd grown older and was on his own more he had come to understand the power his light skin gave him to hide who he was among strangers.

George was nearly fourteen now, six years since the Garlands had moved to St. Louis from Virginia, bringing with them a handful of slaves, including George, his mother Lizzy, and his grandmother Aggy. George had been born in a small town in North Carolina, where Mr. Burwell, his mother's master, had sent her to be the slave of his eldest son, Robert, a minister who had just married. Lizzy was miserable being separated from Aggy and the rest of her slave family. And she hated North Carolina for another reason: It was there that Alexander Kirkland, a wealthy member of Robert's congregation, first saw Lizzy. While Robert looked the other way, Kirkland made Lizzy his concubine, and after four years, George was born.

The North Carolina Burwells sent Lizzy and George back to the family in Virginia, where they were reunited with Aggy, when George was only a few months old. The Virginia Burwells always said Lizzy was sent back to avoid the disgrace she had brought on the small-town minister and his wife with her white-skinned, newborn son. Well, his mother hadn't wanted him, he knew that.

George didn't think Mistress Anne, a daughter of Armistead Burwell, or her husband, Master Hugh Garland, minded much what happened in North Carolina. The

George's mother, Elizabeth Hobbs Keckly.
Wood engraving, 1868. MHS Library.

Garlands were more than happy to have Lizzy as their slave. Anyone could see how valuable she had become to them. Even though Mr. Garland was a lawyer, the family mostly lived off Lizzy's earnings from her work as a hired-out dressmaker for the wealthiest St. Louis women. George knew he was valuable, too. He was a clever boy—he could read and write—and mostly cooperative.

George decided to loop downhill toward the river on his way over to his master's law office. On Locust Street, he passed the slave pens owned by Mr. Lynch, one of the town's slave dealers. Inside, slaves who were waiting to be bought and sold were locked up. He turned his head away as he walked by. As he neared the docks, he heard a familiar voice call his name. It was his friend William. Twelve years old, William had recently been hired out to help Mr. Lynch at auction. It was Mr. Lynch who taught William how to cheat buyers by blackening the hair of older slaves.

Now William was panting and shaking all over his body. George had never seen his friend look so panicked, and at first he couldn't make out what William was trying to tell him. Something about Mr. Lynch and a sale. "Slow down, William. I can't understand you!" George told his friend.

"I heard Mr. Lynch talking to Master James"—James Wilson was the lawyer who owned William, his younger

Men waiting to purchase slaves at Lynch's Slave Market, 104 Locust Street.
Daguerreotype by Thomas Easterly, ca. 1852.
MHS Photographs and Prints.

brother, John, and their mother, Nancy. William tried to hold back his tears, but his brown cheeks were already wet. "Master James wants to sell. . . ."

"Sell who?" George cried.

"John or me, I'm not sure, I'm not sure!" At this, William began heaving great gulps of air.

George was stunned. How could this be? He had heard Master James was a good man. "Are you sure he's really selling?" he asked his friend.

William moaned. "Ohhhh, I think so . . . I don't know. I heard them talking. Master James needs money! They were talking about 'Nancy's boy!'"

"Come with me!" George grabbed William's arm and started steering him back toward the Garland house. Miss Anne, George's mistress, knew Nancy and liked her. Maybe she would talk to Master Hugh, he thought. Then Master Hugh could talk to Master James.

When they reached the house, which stood on Olive Street, they ran around back and into the kitchen. There they found Miss Anne and Aggy, George's grandmother, shelling peas at the kitchen table.

"What is all this?" Miss Anne asked. She had a face pinched with endless worry, brought on mostly by the family's money troubles.

"Miss Anne!" George began, catching his breath. "William heard Master James talking to Mr. Lynch about selling him or his brother away!"

Mrs. Garland shifted uncomfortably in her seat. This was just the kind of dirty business that made slavery ugly, even to a slaveholder. In her heart, she truly believed that no one she knew ever liked to break up families. In fact, most of the people she knew had lost money avoiding separating mothers from children. But sometimes, surely, it was impossible to avoid. She had heard about James Wilson's debts.

"What am I supposed to do?" she asked, sharply. Aggy glanced at her quickly, then looked back at her hands as she went on with her peas. Miss Anne wished she hadn't been told about this. It made her uncomfortable. Suddenly, she thought to ask George what he had been doing out of the house. It made her feel immediately better to be able to take charge again. "What have you been up to?" she asked.

The papers for Mr. Norris! George had forgotten all about them. In horror, he realized he didn't know where they were. He must have dropped them somewhere in the street. "What have you been up to, you lazy boy? Now tell me the truth!" Miss Anne said, fretfully. Aggy's hands kept moving swiftly.

There was no use trying to get Miss Anne to talk to Master Hugh now. The tears fell silently down William's cheeks as he saw George's fear and confusion. Aggy's eyes met William's. Poor boy, she seemed to want to say.

Instead of answering Mrs. Garland, George turned and ran out of the kitchen, and William ran after him. He had to find those papers. But most of all, he had to help his best friend.

Chapter 2

The Stowaway

*T*he only thing George could think to do was retrace his steps down to the river to where he'd run into William. William walked back with him partway, but he had to go home to his master's house. When he turned to go, George told him was sorry. He had messed up. "But I promise I'll think of something," he said. Privately, he knew that if he couldn't find those papers, Master Hugh would be furious with him and in no mood to help a slave. In general, Master Hugh was a gentle, scholarly man, but, like all slaveholders, he knew others who would punish his slaves for him if he didn't have the will or strength to do it himself. George vividly remembered the day one of Mr. Garland's slaves, a man named Chapman, went away with a strange man and came back the next day with raw welts on his back.

In his thirteen years, George had seen more than enough to know what slavery really was. Master Hugh once sold a man for a single dollar to have his debts forgiven by the purchaser. George's mother had often told him the story of when she was a little girl in Virginia and watched the local slave dealer put a little boy, one of her playmates, whose mother was the Burwell family cook, on a hanging scale to weigh him and set his sale price, as if he were a bag of flour being sold by the pound. All the tears in the world wouldn't have stopped that sale because Master Burwell needed the money to pay for his hogs for the winter. Then, fed up with the mother's weeping, Mr. Burwell finally punished her. "You've got to smile 'em to death to win," his mother once said. "But you bide your time and it will come, and when it does, you take it, and *do* for yourself." George wasn't sure exactly what she meant. It felt more like a curse than advice to have to wait to just *be*. All the white boys he knew could be themselves. Wasn't he as white as any of them? Why did *he* have to pretend to be a nobody?

As he walked along the dusty streets, George scanned the ground looking for the bundle of papers he was sure he must have dropped somewhere. He stopped several men along the way to ask if they'd seen the papers, but no one had. He even went into some of the shops in case someone had brought them inside. He wasn't sure what to do. If he came home empty-handed, he would have to confess right away that he didn't know where the papers were because he wouldn't have the letter Mr. Norris was supposed to give him. But if he went to Mr. Norris and pretended he had just come for the letter, he might be able to bring it back anyway and at least have more time to find out what happened to the papers. This is what he decided to do.

Mr. Norris was working in the second-floor law office on Locust Street, which he shared with Mr. Garland, when George knocked softly on the door. An elderly black man George had seen before opened the door to let him in. George suddenly couldn't remember whether Mr. Norris owned the man or hired him—and if he hired him, who owned him. Suddenly, it seemed important to know. Mr. Norris would never have hired a free black man. Men like Mr. Garland and Mr. Norris didn't want to support the free black people of St. Louis in any way. In their view, too many free blacks in a community ruined the few good slaves who were left, making them uppity and unruly.

"George!" Mr. Norris greeted him, in a friendly way. "What have you to give me today?" George was stumped for a few seconds and stood silently, head down. "Nothing just yet, sir," he finally answered. "But Master Garland sent me to pick up a letter."

"Oh, yes. Here it is." Mr. Norris pointed to a long envelope on his desk. "I'll be over at the Garlands' for supper later anyway, and Mr. Garland can give me what he has then."

George reached over to pick up the letter. He glanced at the writing on the front—it was addressed to Mr. Garland—then dropped his hand self-consciously when he noticed Mr. Norris looking at him. "You can read, I know," Mr. Norris said. "Nothing wrong with that. Useful at times. I'm not one of those who wants my slaves ignorant. Can't read your Bible if you can't read at all. Can you write, too?" he asked George. George nodded in reply. With his master's permission, his mother had taught him to read and write. "That's pushing it a bit," Mr. Norris said. "But your master has some funny Virginia ways, I guess." By now George just wanted to leave. He didn't like talking to Mr. Norris—or any white man—more than was necessary, and he certainly didn't like talking with him about whether he could read or write.

Once outside, George's mind raced forward to the inevitable moment only an hour or so away when Mr. Norris would ask Master Hugh for the papers and Master Hugh would ask George what he did with them. In his panic, he found himself naturally going down to the river. It was the Mississippi River—its flowing waters, driving steamboats, and bustling docks—that always calmed him. The river promised a world elsewhere—a life he had heard of where no one was a slave. Dreamily, he looked over to the far side of the river, to the banks of Illinois. Somewhere in the middle of the river was an invisible line that divided the state of Missouri from the state of Illinois. Once you crossed that line you were in free territory. Steamboats crossed that line every minute of every day, and a ferryboat went back and forth between the banks. What if he could stow away on a steamboat and be taken far away? He wouldn't care where he went, he told himself, as long as it was north. The only thing that kept him back was his mother and his grandmother. They would break their hearts in worrying about what happened to him.

St. Louis levee.
Daguerreotype by Thomas Easterly, 1853.
MHS Photographs and Prints.

But that was not the only reason to hesitate, he knew. The law of the land said that any runaway found in the North must be captured and returned to his or her master. That meant that in no state in the United States could a runaway slave live free and in the clear. "It's all one big slave pen!" he had heard the slave Chapman say in disgust one evening when a few of the neighborhood slaves were gathered in the Garland slave quarters. "Run here, run there, it's lock you up and bring you down."

"That's why we have to buy our freedom," George's mother had answered, softly. As usual, over her lap was draped the skirt or bodice or cape she was sewing for some white lady in town. The fabric fell over the floor in luxuriant folds. George had been watching his mother intently. She sat with her back straight, refusing to bend to her work and risk hurting her neck and back like the other seamstresses she knew. She had dignity and determination, and the other slaves listened to her carefully. "Nobody can take away what's *legally* yours," she had continued. "They don't respect your rights as a human being, but they respect property. Own yourself and even they can't say they own you."

By this point in his reverie, George was standing on one of the docks, leaning over a railing, looking out at the river. Nothing looked so easy as to hop on a steamboat. There was one docked nearby, the *Natchez*, bumping gently against the wooden planks. It looked empty of passengers and cargo just then, but no doubt would be filled up and ready for a voyage by the next day. Without really thinking, George darted down to the edge of the dock and raced up the narrow plank that ran to the boat. He'd never been on a steamboat before and had no idea of how to get below deck, so he took the first hiding place that offered itself—behind a stack of barrels piled at one end of the deck. Crouching down with his knees to his eyes and his nose pressed to one of the barrels, he tried to get comfortable. He would wait until it grew dark, he thought, and then look for a better place to hide.

Chapter 3

Returning Home

George must have been sleeping, because he was lying down, with his legs stretched out from behind the barrels, when he became aware of the smell of smoke overhead. Opening his eyes, he saw a man smoking a cigar standing over him.

"Now, who are you?" the man asked. Behind his head, the sky was dark with a smattering of brightly glistening stars. George jumped to his feet. "I was tired and fell asleep," he said.

"I can see that," the man answered, pointing his cigar to where George had been lying to make the point. "Don't you think you'd better be getting home?" The man put his cigar back in his mouth and leaned down to squint at George. "Won't your mama be missing you?" he continued.

"I don't have a mama," George lied. "She died in the cholera of '49, and I had to go live with my aunt."

"Then won't your aunt be wondering where you are?" The man seemed unmoved by George's dead mother. "What's your name?"

"Louis," he said. That was the name of the Garlands' two-year-old son, and the first name that came to George's mind. "Louis Kirkland."

"Well, Louis Kirkland," said the cigar-smoking man. "You can't be meaning to stay here all night, and I'm sure your aunt will want to find you home." He gave George a light shove toward the edge of the boat.

"No, sir. I mean yes, sir," George replied. "I'll be going, I guess, sir." The plank was still down, and as he walked over it, George looked back at the man, who had turned away and was staring across the river, a red ember flickering at the tip of his cigar. George supposed that the man had thought he was a white boy likely running away from home. He certainly hadn't acted like George was a runaway slave. In fact, George realized, he hadn't acted like a runaway slave, falling asleep. Some escape! What did he think he was doing, he asked himself as he turned his steps toward the Garlands'. Was he crazy? What was he going to tell Mr. Garland now? Or his mother, for that matter? And what was he thinking giving Kirkland as his name? That was a secret game he played with himself, calling himself by his slaveholding father's name, "Kirkland." He'd never actually tried to use the name. Mr. Kirkland probably didn't remember that George existed, if he'd ever known in the first place. George berated himself all the way home.

A further accusatory thought rose up to trouble him as well, although he didn't like to admit it to himself. In worrying about his own situation, he had forgotten completely about his best friend, William. He had been more afraid of being punished by Mr. Garland than concerned about saving William from something much worse—being sold away. In thinking of himself, he had been willing to break his promise to his friend.

Suddenly, he thought of Mr. Norris's letter and felt in his pocket to make sure he hadn't lost that, too. Fortunately, the letter was still there, although bent at the corners and slightly soiled.

He did not know how long he'd been asleep, but he hoped it hadn't been too long. When he reached the house, the front windows were dark. He went around to the back to where the slave quarters stood and saw by a light in her window that his mother wasn't asleep.

Lizzy's first reaction upon seeing her son was joy— George could see that in her face—but joy quickly passed to anger. "Where have you been?" she demanded. "Where have you been?"

"I fell asleep down by the docks," he said. He didn't want to tell her he had boarded a steamboat, a steamboat that might have sailed away with him on it. As it was, his mother could not believe her ears. She grabbed George by the arm and shook him furiously.

"You what? Fell asleep? What do you mean?" She began hitting him on the side of his head. "Do you know what I've been going through?" She hit him. "Do you know what I thought?" She hit him. "Can you even imagine?" Another hit. "That you were hurt? Or dead? Or kidnapped? Or run away?" After each question she hit him again. "Do you understand how this looks to Master Hugh? Do you have any idea how hard it is to get them to trust you, to believe you? Do you understand me?" Hit. Hit. Hit.

George had not even tried to duck away from the blows. He knew that all his mother said was true. He knew that she was exhausted by work and worry. The two looked at each other for a few seconds. Lizzy was crying, but George's eyes were dry.

"I won't ever do this to you again," he said. At that, she took him in her arms and began rocking him gently.

"I'm sorry," she said, rocking him.

His mother told him that about a month ago she had asked Master Hugh to sell her their freedom and that he had flatly refused. He also told Lizzy never to ask him again.

"Why didn't you tell me?" George asked. He now understood how his disappearance even for a few hours could damage his mother's plans to win Master Hugh's consent to her proposal.

"I didn't want to raise your hopes and then have you be disappointed," she answered. George didn't know what to say. "But don't think I'm done asking," she said, smiling.

Before going to bed that night, George told his mother about William and the slave trader. She promised she'd think of something to do to help. He didn't tell her about Master Hugh's papers or the letter he still had in his pocket. He did not want to give her another reason to be disappointed and angry with him.

Chapter 4

The Auction Block

*M*r. Garland didn't ask George where he had been the night before, not even when George handed him Mr. Norris's letter. Instead, he told George to see if Miss Anne had any errands for him and if not, to go help Chapman. "I'm going to court today," he said. George could not understand why Master Hugh had let him alone, but he certainly wasn't going to stay around to argue with his luck. Mrs. Garland, however, was not so distracted that she forgot that George had not helped serve supper the night before. But fortunately for George, little Louis, the Garlands' youngest, took the opportunity of George's appearance in the kitchen to launch himself into a violent temper tantrum, demanding his mother's attention. "Aggy! Aggy!" Anne called, while she tried to quiet the child. In the midst of the uproar, George escaped.

He found Chapman, or Chap, outside harnessing the Garlands' old horse to a cart to haul firewood back to the house. George liked Chap immensely. He was a steady, burly, dark-skinned man, about thirty-five years old, who had come to St. Louis from Virginia with the family. Mr. Garland's father had loaned Chap to Master Hugh when he moved, but then sold him the slave for one dollar not long after the family settled in St. Louis. Chap had been forced to leave behind a wife and small son in Virginia, and he vowed that one day he would go back to see them. A story had gone

A slave father sold away from his family.
Wood engraving, 1859. MHS Library.

around among the slaves that he had once tried to run away to Virginia—and that was why he had been whipped—but Mr. Garland seemed to place so much faith in him that George doubted the story was true. By now, it had been six years since Chap had seen his family, and although he never mentioned them, he'd taken a special liking to George, who was about the age of his own son.

George climbed up next to Chap, who turned the horse away from the house. They drove silently for a few minutes. Finally, Chap asked George what had happened to him the night before. "Your mama told the white folks that you were feeling sick and staying in bed," he told George. "But she was the one who was sick—with worry." George wanted to tell someone the truth. It was hard to keep so much to himself. He could trust Chap, he felt, so he told him everything: about William, the lost papers, and almost running away. If Chap was surprised, he did not show it. Instead, George's story seemed to make him sad.

"I don't blame you for doing what you did," Chap said. "It's a natural feeling. I sometimes hate myself for staying put." They were just then driving past the courthouse. Outside stood the whipping post where slaves were regularly punished and, nearby, the auction block where slaves were displayed for sale. Several white men were milling around, as if expecting a sale to take place soon. It sickened George to see. He imagined William standing on the block in a group of slaves who were up for sale, with these very men looking them over, like horses. The slaves would be expected to do whatever they were told by the agent to help the sale along: open their mouths so that their teeth could be checked or take off their clothes to be examined for signs of illness or injury. It didn't matter how young or old the slave was, man or woman, boy or girl.

"How can a *man* put up with that?" Chap said, his eyes fixed on the auction block. "You're right to feel the way you do, and I admire you for it. These are hard times," he went on. "The Reverend Overall says that the more scared the white man is of us, the worse he treats us." George knew the Reverend Isaac Overall. He had been a slave until two years earlier, when his master died and the widow gave him his freedom. A short, stocky man, the preacher drove a dray cart to earn a living because he didn't have his own church. His cart was his pulpit, he liked to say. "And these are hard times," Chap repeated. "Harder than I've ever seen."

They were coming in sight of the market, where firewood, wool, cotton, and other goods unloaded at the docks were sold. George climbed down off the cart after Chap and followed him into the crowd. The market was filled with people. Many were strangers to St. Louis, visitors from nearby Kentucky, Indiana, and Illinois who came to the big city regularly for business or pleasure. Some were on their way to glamorous, exotic New Orleans, where one could see the latest fashions

Slaves on their way to market to purchase goods for their masters.
Wood engraving after Edwin Austen Abbey, 1875. MHS Library.

or buy costly imports from Europe. Recently, large numbers of German and Irish immigrants had flooded into St. Louis, and George could pick out their accents among the dozens of men, women, and children milling about.

Chap and George loaded up the cart and began the drive home. They passed the courthouse a second time. It was midday, and now a group of men were clustered around the auction block. On the platform, Mr. Lynch, the slave dealer, stood talking to a man in a bowler hat. George recognized Lynch instantly, but didn't know the other man. Then he saw William and his brother, John. The boys were standing a little off to the side, behind Mr. Lynch. They were dressed in their Sunday clothes and holding hands. And then George heard it. A wail unlike anything he had ever heard in his life. Searching the courthouse grounds to find the source of this unearthly sound, he saw Nancy on her knees, clutching the coat of her master, Mr. Wilson.

George rose to leap off the cart, but Chap held him fast. "Leave it alone!" he said, gruffly. "What good will you running in there do?"

"Let go!" George shrieked. He yanked away from Chap, leapt off the cart, and ran toward Mr. Wilson, who was trying to shove Nancy back to the ground. She clung desperately to the side of his coat, hanging on with all her weight, and the closer George came, the clearer he could hear her cries. "Oh, Master John! Oh, master! Please! Spare my sons. Oh, please! Don't sell them. I'll die. I will! Oh, my God! Oh, my God! Please have mercy!" Nothing George had ever heard before was as heart-wrenching to him as Nancy's cries, and as long as he lived he would never forget the sound of her despair. In her frenzy to not let go, Nancy had allowed herself to be dragged across the ground, and her knees were cut and bleeding.

Suddenly, Mr. Lynch appeared at Mr. Wilson's side.

"Dr. Farrar will buy one of the boys," Mr. Lynch said.

"Whichever one you want to sell to him, seeing as they're both the same price."

"You hear that, Nancy?" Mr. Wilson said. "Now get up off your knees and dry your eyes! You can have one of the boys *guaranteed* in town. And, see? I'll even let you decide which one."

Slave children could be sold away from their parents at any time.
Wood engraving, 1859. MHS Library.

George froze. Dr. Farrar was married to one of the Garland daughters, and George knew him well because he was often called in to take care of the family slaves. George wondered if Mistress Anne, or maybe his mother, had told the Farrars about the sale. Lizzy had nursed the Garland children when they were small, and she still made all of the girls' dresses. She even boasted about how much the Garland children loved her. George reasoned that the man in the bowler hat must be Dr. Farrar's agent, who had been sent to buy one of the boys. Slaveholders preferred using middle men, as it seemed a less dirty business when it was done by someone else.

Nancy had grown quiet while Mr. Wilson spoke, but her eyes were wild. "Both," she said, rising to her feet. "He has to take both," she continued, her voice growing stronger and firmer. "That was what you promised. That you would sell them together!"

Mr. Wilson looked at Mr. Lynch, who glanced coolly in Nancy's direction, but without seeing her, then back to Mr. Wilson. "Farrar can't afford both," Mr. Lynch said.

"Hey!" called a voice from the group of men on the courthouse lawn. "Is there a sale here, today? I can't keep waiting all day!"

"Yes, hold on," Mr. Lynch called back. "Just doing some business, then we'll be starting."

Mr. Wilson turned to look at Nancy, who now looked him steadily in the eye. It was as if she were challenging him to break this one, single promise, challenging him with all her years of servitude—every act she had ever performed for this man—every meal she had cooked, shirt she had washed, floor she had swept, or Wilson infant she had helped his wife bring into this world and nurse and raise—daring him to turn his back on her in the only promise she had ever extracted from him. He turned away from her gaze.

"Wait on one; sell the other," he told Lynch. "It's the best I can do, Nancy," he said, softly. "You'll see him, you know that. The Farrars are a good family and will treat him well."

"Which one?" Mr. Lynch asked. Mr. Wilson shrugged. "Look," Mr. Lynch finally said. "Keep William. He can continue to work for me, and you know my money's good."

George, who had heard the whole transaction, turned to look at William, who still stood on the auction block, holding his brother's hand. Both boys were looking at their mother, Mr. Lynch, and Mr. Wilson.

George looked around. Chap had not moved the cart an inch, but had sat waiting for George. Chap was not looking at the scene that had taken place on the courthouse lawn, but away toward the river. He was thinking of his long-lost wife and son.

George walked back to the cart and, without saying a word, climbed up next to Chap, and they rode the rest of the way home without speaking.

Chapter 5

Escape

Mr. Garland was preoccupied with the slavery case he was handling—the one having to do with the slave couple, Dred and Harriet Scott—which had come to a head the day of the sale of Nancy's son. It was widely discussed in the slave quarters how the Scotts were suing their owner, a widow named Mrs. Emerson, for their freedom because they had lived with her husband in free territory for a few years. The fact that living in free territory gave a slave claim to being free naturally interested St. Louis slaves, who frequently traveled on the ferry to Illinois and back. Lizzy and Chap had crossed the river, and returned, many times on their own. Other slaves George knew had been as far as New York or Boston with their masters, who liked traveling with their favorite slaves. They came back with amazing stories about what it was like in the big, northern cities.

Dred Scott, a slave who sued for freedom after living in a free state.
Photograph of daguerreotype, 1857. MHS Photographs and Prints.

On the day Nancy's son John was sold, the Missouri Supreme Court ruled in favor of Mrs. Emerson, and for the next few weeks, George noticed, Mr. Garland seemed less fretful than usual. Certainly, Chap was right about the state of things. Times *were* hard. The judges decided in Mrs. Emerson's favor because of what they saw as a dark antislavery spirit in the land, which made them feel that it was not a good time for a slaveholding state like Missouri to do anything that looked antislavery, such as granting the Scotts their freedom.

A man in Master Hugh's position could not be seen as antislavery either, so he would never sell Lizzy her freedom, or her son's. This idea took hold of George one afternoon not many days after witnessing his friend's close call at the auction block. It was a thought that cast a terrible shadow over his mind. Nothing would ever change for him, he realized. He would live out his life a slave, like Aggy, who was born a slave and would die a slave. George had never felt so hopeless before.

Despite George's dark mood, life seemed to settle back to normal. Nancy was quiet, William continued working for Mr. Lynch, and John went to live with the Farrars as their slave. Lizzy went out every day except Sundays to sew for her lady clients, coming home at night tired and subdued. Aggy helped Mistress Anne in the kitchen and with the younger children in the nursery. The married Garland daughters,

Molly and Carrie, visited nearly every day. Master Hugh went to his law office to work. George did the chores around the house, ran errands, and helped Chap with the heavy work.

George learned that it was his mother who had talked to Carrie, who was now Mrs. Farrar, about buying John. Lizzy had a great influence over the Garland daughters, whom she had helped raise.

Then one day Chap told George he wanted to talk to him about something important.

"I need your help," Chap said. "But you can't tell anyone, not even your mother."

This request startled George. Not that he told his mother everything, but to have Chap tell him to keep a secret from her was unusual. Chap was a serious man, not given to games or surprises. He must have felt strongly, otherwise he never would have approached George in this way.

"I need you to bring this to William tonight," said Chap, showing George a small bundle, wrapped in a blue cloth.

"What is it?" George asked.

"If I tell you, it'll only get you in trouble."

George wasn't sure what to say. He trusted Chap—that is, as much as he trusted anyone. One lesson he had learned as a slave was how hard it was to trust anyone, even other slaves. Lizzy always said you could never depend on anyone, except yourself. Although she had friends among the slaves, George could see how much his mother kept herself apart.

But George did not want to disappoint Chap, who, as far back as George could remember, had been like a father to him. And Chap had never, until that moment, asked him to do anything for him.

"Okay," George said.

"Good," Chap said. "You need to go as soon as it's dark. And quietly. Try not to draw attention to yourself. If you are stopped, you can say you're visiting a sick friend. But above all, keep moving."

For an instant, George wondered if he were being asked to do this because he looked white and was less likely to be stopped in the streets at night than a black man, like Chap. The idea thrilled him. It gave him a kind of power.

"Okay," he said, again. He took the bundle.

His mother and grandmother were asleep when he slipped out of the cabin they shared and began his walk to the Wilson house slave quarters, where William and Nancy lived, going by alleyways and back streets as much as possible.

He had no sooner knocked than William opened the door and pulled him inside. He had been waiting for George to arrive. Nancy was out.

"What is going on?" George asked.

"Chap gave you that?" William asked, reaching for the bundle.

"Yes," George said, handing it to his friend. "What is it, William? What's going on?"

William untied the string that held the bundle together, spreading its contents on the table. George could see some clothing and papers.

"What is it?" he asked William.

"We're leaving," William said. At first, George didn't understand what William meant. "Leaving" didn't make sense to him as something a slave did. Free folks "left" to move to other cities, they "left" to visit friends in other towns. They left and came back, or not, as they wished. Slaves did not leave. They were pushed and pulled by their masters, dragged far away from kith and kin against their will, forced to "leave."

"Leaving?" George asked.

"Running away," William whispered, almost ferociously. He looked closely at his friend. "We're taking John. It's all planned out. I can't tell you everything."

In her desperation to keep her family together, Nancy had decided they had to run away. It was a rare and dangerous path she had chosen. Most runaways were young men, and most runaways fled alone. The Fugitive Slave Law dictated that runaway slaves be hunted and returned to their owners. A family that ran away together was at greater risk of capture. In such cases, there was danger in numbers.

George looked again at the bundle. There was clothing to change into so Mr. Wilson couldn't tell the slave catchers what the slaves were wearing when he discovered they

Running away was dangerous for a slave, but especially for a slave family.
Wood engraving by Van Ingen Snyder, 1864. MHS Library.

were missing. Forged passes stated their master had given them permission to travel alone, in case they were stopped. Letters directed them to people in the North—black and white—who were known to be helpful to runaway slaves. These good people hid runaways in their cellars and attics, supplying them with food, shelter, and rest before directing them on their way, to the next stop, farther north.

George had heard about the underground railroad that ran through St. Louis. There were slaves and free blacks who marked their fences to signal to runaways where they could find something to eat. He had heard that there was a dirt crawl space beneath the basement floor of the Reverend Berry's church where runaways hid before moving on. He and William had talked about how long a runaway could hide in a dirt cellar. William had thought weeks, at most. You could become blind and crippled if you spent too much time hiding in a dirt crawl space. George had said years, as long as you had food and water. Neither liked the idea of the snakes and lizards they imagined you'd have to share such a hideaway with.

"You should get going," William told him. "You shouldn't stay here."

George knew William was right, but he didn't want to go. He felt suddenly depressed by the thought of saying good-bye to his friend, knowing he might never see him again. He wondered if he was being selfish. Shouldn't he be happy that William was escaping? Then he realized he wished he were going with him, and that was the real reason he was depressed.

"You'll get away, too," said William, as if reading his mind. "Your mother will take care of that. That's what my mother says." He gave George a slight shove.

"Maybe. Maybe not," George answered.

George left without really saying good-bye. He didn't know what to say to William. He was confused about his feelings. He didn't want Nancy, William, and John to stay, but he didn't want them to go. As he hurried home, his head tucked down under a slight drizzle, he felt as if his heart were bursting. For the first time in his life, he wished that he were white. He felt ashamed of himself, but it was true.

He walked home, thinking. Well, why wasn't he white? His father was white. *Both* grandfathers were white. But this isn't the way things are, he thought bitterly.

Chapter 6

Helping Fugitives

After Nancy, William, and John were discovered missing, Dr. Farrar and Mr. Wilson printed a circular announcing a $300 reward for information leading to the capture of "the negro woman Nancy and her two boys." They took out ads in the local papers. But no trace of the fugitives could be found.

When George tried to talk with Chap about how they escaped, Chap refused to answer his questions. "The less you know, the better," Chap said. George understood that Chap was trying to protect him, but he didn't want to be protected in this way. He wanted to understand how it worked. He suspected that Chap played a large part in spiriting them away.

Chap and Lizzy disagreed about the way to freedom. She would never think of running away. It wasn't a sure way, she'd argue. Besides, she thought of it like stealing, something degrading. No, she was going to buy herself and George. Chap would say back that it wasn't stealing, when your master had no right to own you in the first place. "You can't steal yourself," he'd say.

George was getting disgusted with the grown-ups' talk. Just *talk* about freedom. If he could help others run away, why didn't Chap run away himself? George could not understand it. One night he asked Chap this very question. Chap grew very quiet before answering, "Because I got nobody to run to, anymore."

"What do you mean?" George asked.

"Just that." Chap stopped speaking. George practically held his breath. He'd never heard Chap talk about his family before. "My son died—last year—scarlet fever. My wife. . . ." He stopped, again. His eyes grew glazed, as if he were looking far away, or maybe nowhere. "She killed herself. *Drowned herself*." He spit out the last two words. "Your mother's friend, Keckly, told me."

James Keckly was the free black man who wanted to marry Lizzy. They had known each other in Virginia, and he had followed Lizzy to St. Louis to propose. When she refused, telling him she could never marry anyone until she was free, James Keckly went back to Virginia. But he'd shown up again a few weeks back. George did not like him.

Several weeks later, Chap asked George to make another delivery of clothes and papers to another runaway. It was a man who had come up from Arkansas. Over the next few months Chap asked George to make his third, then his fourth and fifth deliveries. Each time his instructions were the same: Rap on the door three times, hand the bundle to whoever answers the door, but don't ask questions and don't linger. Use back alleys and deserted streets to reach your destination and return home as quickly as you can. For luck, George always wore the same blue shirt his mother had sewn for him.

Chap never told George much about the fugitives. He never again recognized any of the people he gave the bundles to. But George quickly realized that there was a whole network of St. Louis blacks like Chap willing to take risks to help others escape. He felt proud that Chap had decided he could trust him. Soon word came back from New York that Nancy, William, and John had arrived safely into the hands of friends.

Months passed, and it was approaching Christmas when one night George's mother confronted him about what he'd been doing for the runaways.

"I know what's going on, Georgie," she said. "I'm not deaf, dumb, and blind. I know all about it. Known for months and I let you do it. But Chap is Chap. This is what he's decided to *do*. It's not your work."

"What do you mean?" George asked.

"This is his *mission*," she answered. "How he answers the

call to do something for his people. A call most of us feel, sooner or later. But he has lost everything, you know, and we haven't," she said.

"But this is what I want to do, too!" George said. He started pacing around the small room, waving his arms. "You don't understand! I hate it here. Everything about it. I know I'm not supposed to, that I'm supposed to feel grateful to the Garlands and all the rest. I know you do. And grandma, too. But I don't! I hate them all!" Against his will, he had started to cry.

"*I* feel grateful?" his mother said. "I've *supported* this family ever since I came here! Grateful? They told me I'd never be worth my salt! But here I am, and they couldn't live without me." She shook her head. "Don't you think I'm unhappy, too? Don't you think I hate this . . . all this . . . hate slavery? My whole life! Nothing but work all day and all night for the white family. But you are right about one thing, Georgie. I don't hate them, and I don't blame them. I've hated others, but I don't hate them."

George wanted to ask his mother whom she hated. Did she hate her white father? Did she hate his white father? He was sure she did.

"I don't want you to do this again," she said.

"What if I want to?" he asked.

"I don't want you to," she repeated. "It's because of what I've told you before. I want to *buy* our freedom. I want Mr.

Garland to agree to sell us. I want to see him agree, with my own eyes. But if you do this, and you're caught, it will never happen. George, listen." Lizzy's dark, deep-set eyes looked suddenly to her son like bottomless pools of pain and longing. George realized that he'd never know all that those eyes had seen and could see still. That because of her, he would never suffer as she had suffered.

"I *dream* about freedom, Georgie. I dream about it. And it's nothing like this. It's like I was born on the wrong side of some window I can look through but can't pass through. And it's all there, on the other side—life, freedom, another world. I'm telling you," her voice grew firmer. "I will not let us live and die as slaves. No, sir. I know I am every bit as smart as the white folks. I know you are, too."

Chapter 7

Household Tragedy

The holiday season came, but there was not much celebrating in the Garland household. Mrs. Garland wrote a letter to her sister lamenting the family's poverty and confessing that she didn't even have a cent to send to the market. Mr. Garland could not seem to earn enough, no matter what he did. Lizzy was still bringing her wages to him, and he tried hiring out Chap for a time. He even contemplated selling his beloved library, which held hundreds of precious books, but his wife persuaded him to spare himself that agony. Nothing seemed to help for long, anyway. The winter was cold, wet, and dismal.

Then one day in the new year, George came upon Master Hugh sitting in his library holding his head in his hands. He did not stir when George walked in, but sat, motionless.

"Master Hugh?" George asked. "Are you all right?"

Mr. Garland lifted his head and looked at George, but the puzzled expression on his face was as if he did not recognize his slave. Finally, he spoke.

"Yes, George. I'm fine. But Louis is sick. Maybe you can run upstairs and see if Miss Anne needs anything from the druggist."

Sickness was a common occurrence in the Garland household. Someone—either a slave, a child, or Miss Anne or Master Hugh himself—was always sick. When the case was bad, Dr. Farrar would arrive carrying his black bag. But mostly, Miss Anne just sent George to the drugstore on Main Street to bring back vials of syrups, pills, ointments, and other concoctions. The slaves had their own remedies of herbs and teas for ailments, except in dire cases, when they, too, were looked at by Dr. Farrar.

George, however, sensed something more urgent than the usual bout of illness as he climbed the wooden stairs to the top-floor nursery. He heard hushed whisperings coming from the room, then the racking cough of the sick boy.

"George!" Aggy was sitting by the boy's bedside, propping him up with her arm, and trying to get him to spit into a pan she held under his pale, contorted face. "Take that outside and fill it with water." George grabbed the metal bucket. A water pump stood on every block. Pumping as fast and as hard as he could, he filled the bucket with the water, which was brown and odorous, until it was too heavy to carry; then he sloshed some water off the top and lugged it back toward the house and upstairs. He was out of breath by the time he came to the top landing.

Aggy dipped a rag into the water and wiped it across Louis's brow. It was then that George noticed Miss Anne sitting in the corner, staring at her son who was at that moment gasping for breath.

"Oh, save him, please save him," she repeated over and over. She had her arms gripped around her chest and was rocking back and forth.

"Yes, Miss Anne," Aggy said soothingly, but kept her attention on the boy.

George thought of the many times he'd helped watch Louis play when his grandmother was sewing or in the kitchen with Miss Anne. Louis took after his father— he was gentle and sensitive, and George found it an easy thing to look after him. Only, once he had done a strange thing, and that was when Louis was only weeks old. George grabbed a handful of dirt from outside, carried it carefully into the nursery, and rubbed it roughly into the baby's scalp. George could not say at the time why he did what he did, but there was something about the boy's soft, downy blond head and milky white skin (George's hair was dark and curly) that provoked him. George remembered the incident itself vaguely, although it was not even three years ago, but he remembered vividly the beating Miss Anne herself gave him when she saw what

George had done. She had grabbed a broom and hit him on his shoulders, back, and legs.

More memorable still, though, was his mother's reaction when George told her what had happened, tears rolling down his cheeks. She started clenching and unclenching her fists rapidly against her skirt. Then she spoke in a voice so low and ferocious he almost didn't recognize it as hers.

"Her mother whipped me, just like that, when I was only five, because of something I did to their baby. Her name was Elizabeth."

"What?" George asked, through his tears.

"Dropped her on the floor when I was taking her out of her cradle. She was fine, nothing happened, she wasn't hurt. It was an accident, of course."

George could not imagine his mother doing something like that to the white family. She hit George sometimes, it was true. But he never saw her do anything against the white folks. She was only five, he told himself, and didn't know what she was doing. But the look in her eyes when she told him the story said otherwise. She knew. It made George feel better, this story of his mother's, and he soon stopped crying. This shared, private store of rage felt precious and fragile to him, something to treasure and protect.

At that instant, while George was thinking of his mother, Louis had another coughing fit. It frightened George to hear such a great gasping sound come from so small a boy. George wanted to be far away, outside. Neither Aggy nor Mistress Anne seemed to be noticing him, so he left the room and ran downstairs. He paused at the door of the library. Master Hugh was bent over a book.

Once outside, George made his way quickly toward the wharves. He wanted to look out at the Mississippi, across to Illinois. Looking across the river always relaxed him. It was times like these he wished William were still there. He missed his friend, the only close friend he had. He thought of the day they found some money in the street and treated themselves to bags of peanuts, which they ate by the river, tossing the shells into the slow, muddy water. They then carefully divided up the change.

The Levee or Landing, St. Louis, Missouri.
Wood engraving by Kilburn, 1857. MHS Library.

Watching the steamboats rocking against the wharf, George thought of the night he ran away and hid on the deck of one of them. Suddenly, he was seized with guilt about the lie he'd told to the white man who found him—that his name was Louis Kirkland. Maybe he put a curse on Louis by using his name. Maybe he stole his spirit that night, like the conjure woman who was said to steal the spirits of white children when their mothers weren't watching.

The clink of chains interrupted George's thoughts. Looking back along the docks, he saw a line of slaves being led by two white men to one of the waiting boats. They were being marched two by two, each slave's ankles shackled with a thick, heavy chain running the length of the line of slaves, binding them together.

George turned away from the line of slaves to look back across the river. Then, with a sigh, he returned home.

By the time he arrived at the Garland house, his mother had returned from the fitting she was doing that afternoon for Mrs. Chouteau, one of her clients. She had relieved Aggy from her post at Louis's bedside and was trying to coax the boy into swallowing some broth. George entered the room silently just as Louis slumped back upon the pillows, sweaty and exhausted. Master Garland was standing at the foot of the bed, staring at his son. Mistress Anne had gone to her own room to lie down and get some rest.

Shackled slaves (left) were often sold south, away from their families.
Wood engraving by Van Ingen Snyder, 1864. MHS Library.

As George stood gazing at the still, deathlike scene, he heard a creaking noise overhead. At first he thought it must have been a mouse or other small animal—no one, as far as he knew, ever went into the tiny attic tucked between the third-floor ceiling and the roof. But then he heard it again, and it sounded nothing like the scurrying feet of a small animal. Instead, it sounded like footsteps.

George's blood chilled. He'd grown up hearing stories about attics haunted by the ghosts of slaves who'd been imprisoned there by their masters. One notorious story, known by everyone he knew, involved a group of slaves who were chained in an attic in New Orleans and burned alive when the house caught on fire. No one thought to rescue them. His mother knew about an attic room in one of the plantation houses in North Carolina, which had a bolt on the outside to keep troublesome slaves locked in. She had told him that you could hear the rustlings of dead slaves who had been whipped in that prison whenever you were in one of the rooms just below.

Over the next three weeks, Louis rallied, then worsened, rallied, then declined. Lizzy suggested they move the boy downstairs, and his parents took him into their own room, setting up a bed for him. During this time, George spent many hours in this room, lighting fires, carrying trays of food and buckets of water. He never again heard the noise from the attic, so he forgot about his fright. Finally, after four weeks of fever and coughing, Louis died. When the child's slight death rattle came, his mother was standing on one side of his bed holding his hand, while Aggy held his hand on the other. His father and Lizzy hovered at the foot of the bed.

George was allowed to attend the funeral. Wearing a smart black jacket his mother sewed for the occasion, he walked beside the horse-driven hearse to the family plot in Bellefontaine Cemetery.

"Where do you think Louis is now?" George asked his mother the night of the funeral. He rarely asked such questions, but Louis's death made him want to know.

"In heaven," she answered.

"Is that where I'll go?" George asked. "The same place?"

"Yes, the same place," his mother assured him. "Black and white to the same place. In heaven, everyone is washed white."

"Then what's wrong with here?" George said. "Why not here?"

"I can't answer you that," she told him. "But heaven is not earth. It puts earth to right."

Not surprisingly, Chap had another view of the matter. "There's a heaven for us and a heaven for them," Chap told George a few days later in answer to his questions. "We couldn't live side by side, not after all that's happened."

George wasn't sure who was right—his mother or Chap—or which he would prefer. If heaven was perfect, then color shouldn't matter, so why shouldn't there be both black and white? Couldn't black be as perfect and clean as white?

Chapter 8

The Price of Freedom

Death came twice more to the Garland family that spring, taking with it the two oldest daughters, Carrie and Molly. Molly died giving birth to a baby girl, who died only days after her mother. Carrie died from a stomach ailment that her desperate husband, Dr. Farrar, could not cure. The sudden death of three of their children and a grandchild all in a row changed Mr. and Mrs. Garland forever. The look of endless worry on Mrs. Garland's face became something more akin to perpetual sorrow. She rarely smiled, and the slightest thing could bring her to tears. Mr. Garland grew even paler, if that were possible. He lost so much weight that his clothes hung from his body, yet he carried himself as if his physical form were now the heaviest of burdens. He walked slowly, stooped forward. Sometimes, when standing up from a chair or climbing stairs, he lost his balance, and more than once, George had to steady him before he fell.

The Garlands also began attending religious services regularly, looking for solace in the peaceful haven of their church. Their slaves sometimes went with them, although they were not allowed to sit with the white family in the main chapel and had to sit in the small balcony with the other slaves and free blacks. George actually preferred those gallery seats, because he liked to look down at the whites seated below. It was much better than being watched from above, he thought.

Not long after the last of the funerals, Lizzy told George that Master Hugh had finally agreed to allow her to buy herself and George from him.

"What about grandma?" George asked, sharply. He had no idea why he felt irritated, but he did. What was wrong with him? Weren't they going to be free?

His mother looked at him closely. "She doesn't want it," Lizzy finally replied, ignoring his tone. "She says she's too old to change her ways." George nodded, but wondered if the truth was that Aggy knew that Lizzy could never afford to buy them all and only said that she didn't want to be free. The price Master Hugh wanted for Lizzy and George alone was already an astronomical sum—$1,200—and George could not see how his mother could pay that. Or maybe it was true. Maybe Aggy didn't care about freedom anymore. George wondered if that's what happens when you're old. He could not recall a single time that Aggy had complained about how the Garlands treated her.

"I told you, didn't I?" Lizzy went on. She was beaming with pleasure and pride. "Now we'll see who's worth her salt."

George was reluctant to tell Chap the news. He was afraid Chap would see their freedom as tainted by the purchase price. But when he told Chap the next afternoon, Chap threw aside the shovel he was holding and congratulated him with a handshake and a loud slap on the back. He had never held it against George that he had obeyed his mother and quit helping the runaways, and now he was genuinely happy for George.

"You'll have to get far away from here," he said to George. He picked up the shovel and leaned on it. "Otherwise, you'll always have the stench of slavery in your nostrils."

But this was not his mother's plan at all, George soon discovered—at least not at first. Her St. Louis sewing business was too good to abandon, and it was how she planned to support herself and her son after they were free. Besides, her lady clients, who admired and trusted her, were going to lend her the money to buy herself and George, and she insisted on working off the debt.

Lizzy also had another plan, which she revealed to George a few days later. This time, she seemed more solemn, and she made him sit down before telling him the news. He could see she was excited beneath the seriousness and hoped he'd be able to give her the response she wanted this time. He didn't want to ruin this conversation the way he had ruined the other one.

But it was impossible for him to feel happy about what she told him—that she was planning to marry Mr. James Keckly. George actually felt sick at the news. He couldn't put his finger on all the things he didn't like about James Keckly. The man seemed frivolous, for one thing, and nothing like his hardworking mother. James cared too much about how he looked and, as far as George could tell, couldn't pass a mirror without staring at himself. He also couldn't understand what the man did with his time, since he never seemed to have to be anywhere and could follow Lizzy clear across the country to woo her. George knew that the feeling was mutual, that James Keckly didn't like him either. James regarded George as an unfortunate necessity of his relationship with Lizzy.

George tried to hide his feelings, but his mother could see them, and this caused a distance between them just at the time—so George thought—when they should have felt a bond, when they could have been celebrating crossing into freedom together. But the wedding came before freedom. The Garlands held a wedding party for Lizzy and James in their own parlor, with family and friends, white and black, invited. Even Aunt Mary, the cook, left the kitchen to come out and celebrate. The guests stood around the parlor, toasting the happy couple and eating strawberries and cream. George kept mostly to himself, brushing off people's congratulations. He ate too much and spent the night awake in bed, overheated and nauseated.

That night, James moved into Lizzy's room. He hung his hat and coat on a hook by the front door. George tried unsuccessfully to ignore them. Fortunately, James was still asleep when George had to leave in the mornings to light the fires throughout the Garland house, and he was generally out visiting friends when George went to bed. The one time James happened to be around at night, George was reading a book that Master Hugh had let him borrow from his library.

"What are you doing, there?" James asked.

"Nothing. Reading," George answered.

James walked over to George and flipped the cover over so he could read the title. He stared at it for a minute, making George wonder if he could actually read. But he could. "Robert Burns: *Poetry*," James read. "Any good?"

"I haven't read it all," George said, pushing the cover back so he could keep reading.

"What you've read. Any good?"

"I like the poems."

"That's good," James said. He sat down on the chair next to George. "Your mother says she wants to send you to school." George had never heard her say that to him. This meant that his mother and James talked about him when he wasn't there. George didn't like the idea of that. If James thought he was going to be George's father, he had another thing coming. "Away to school," James added. "Once she's bought you, she can do that, you know."

And I'll bet that's what you'd like—to send me away, George thought. He had always wanted just to get away, but being kicked out, which is what this felt like, felt different, not what he'd wanted at all.

Not long afterward, Lizzy and James Keckly were allowed to move into some rooms in a house on Fifth Street, leaving George behind. George was both relieved and hurt. He was sure it hadn't been his mother's idea, but she obviously hadn't objected. George spent his evenings with Chap. Chap would whittle a piece of wood while the two chatted, or George read to him from one of Master Hugh's books. They did not talk about what was happening with Lizzy's plans for freedom, because neither of them knew what was going on. But sometimes Chap would go out late at night, without telling George about it. George knew this, because when he woke up in the middle of the night from a bad dream, as he sometimes did, he would look for Chap, and he wasn't always there. It felt to George that he could rely on no one.

About this time, Master Hugh fell ill. He continued to work on his law cases, including his defense of Mrs. Emerson

Hugh Garland.
Steel engraving by J. C. Buttre, 1853. MHS Photographs and Prints.

against the Scotts, but finally, in the fall, he retreated to his bedroom—the room where Louis had died. Again, Aggy and Lizzy were called to sit by the sickbed to help their mistress attend her husband. Again, Dr. Farrar made regular calls. Finally, the day came when Mistress Anne summoned Chap, Aggy, and Lizzy to Master Hugh's bedside. He was dying, and he wanted to say some words of farewell and advice to them.

"Your mistress will take care of you," he said, looking up and around at the three slaves assembled before him. "Just perform your duties faithfully and trust in God." All three took turns shaking his hand. "And George?" Master Hugh said. "Where is George?"

"I'm here, Master." George stepped forward, so that Mr. Garland could see him, although it wasn't clear to George that he could focus his eyes, which seemed glazed and vacant.

"Obey your mistress and your elders. You are restless, but in time, all shall pass. In a little while, we will all be reunited."

"Yes, sir," George said. He was not sure he'd want to be reunited with his master in heaven. In fact, he was pretty sure he did not want it.

Suddenly, the dying man sat up straight in bed and fixed his eyes on something before the window. "Louis!" he said. Anne started. Everyone looked up and around the room.

Then, just as suddenly, Master Hugh sank back on the pillows. "Anne: That will do," Master Hugh said quietly, turning his face to the side. George heard the final release of breath as Mr. Garland died.

It was Miss Anne who finally arranged the sale of Lizzy and George to Lizzy. One of Miss Anne's older brothers came up from Vicksburg to help her settle her husband's estate—to pay off his debts, to collect his legal fees, and to sell off some of his property, including his slaves. Miss Anne had an official bill of sale drawn up for Lizzy's purchase of herself and her son. Lizzy wanted to be sure George saw it, so he would never forget what it cost to make him free. It's not that she wanted him to feel guilty; she wanted him to value freedom. She had sweated blood and tears, she told him, to make them free.

*The actual freedom papers of Elizabeth Keckly and her son, George,
signed by Mrs. Anne Garland.*
November 13, 1855. MHS Archives.

Chapter 9

A Surprise Visitor

*B*eing free changed George's life, at least on the surface of things. He eventually moved in with Lizzy and James. And he found work among a group of black and immigrant laborers on the docks whose job it was to load and unload steamboats. On occasion, a newly arrived traveler, usually a blustering, well-dressed white man, would notice the intelligent-looking George and offer him some change to run an errand or help carry his luggage to a nearby hotel or rooming house.

But life didn't feel that different to George, and he realized that Chap was right. If you don't move away from your enslavement, you never feel yourself free. What was the difference, really? He gave most of his wages to his mother, and he still spent a good deal of time at the Garlands'.

In fact, in the late afternoons, instead of going home to his mother and her new husband, George would head back to the Garlands', where he would share dinner with Chap and Aggy, sometimes in the kitchen, sometimes out back in the cabins.

But one day after work, George decided to go home to his mother's house on Fifth Street. He found James alone in the front room, crouched over the table, drunk and angry.

"What are you doing here?" James demanded, when he saw George.

"Nothing," George said.

"Nothing," James mimicked him. "Nothing. That's what everyone says. That's what your mother says."

George didn't know what James was talking about, and he was pretty sure he didn't want to know. James, on the other hand, sensing George's indifference, seemed eager to explain.

"You think you know your mother, do you? You think anyone knows her? No one. Ever. What's she doing with that Chap fellow?" he asked, suddenly. "They're always talking. Do you know? What?"

Is this where Chap went at night? George wondered. If so, why? The fact that James didn't like it made their visits even more mysterious. James, evidently, was jealous—George could see that. George was also sure there was nothing between his mother and Chap, but he had no particular desire to set James's mind at ease. Let him be jealous, if that's what he is, George thought. But this left the matter of the visits unexplained.

All this while, James had been picking at some food in a bowl on the table in front of him. Suddenly, he stood up and pushed over his chair. It fell to the floor with a loud bang. Lurching toward George, James made a grab for George's collar, but missed and fell forward, into the table, sending the bowl clanging to the floor. George backed off toward one wall.

"You ask your mother what she thinks she's doing!" James screamed in George's direction.

George was stunned. He'd noticed James's drinking before, but he'd never actually seen James drunk—or at any rate, mean drunk. It was as if George were seeing past the happy-go-lucky mask that James usually managed to have pasted to his face. It seemed unthinkable that his hardworking and reserved mother could respect a man like this. George dismissed the idea of even telling his mother about James's disgusting behavior. It had been George's experience that grown-ups did not like being told things that upset their routines or beliefs. George remembered how annoyed Miss Anne seemed when he told her about William being sold, because it contradicted her belief that all slaveholders were kind and good; or how Master Hugh would look when anyone mentioned the emancipation movements in St.

Louis. Master Hugh did not mind emancipationists, as long as they were far away in the North, and in no way threatened to interfere with his, or his neighbors', slaveholding. Obviously, his mother saw something in James Keckly that was beyond George's sight. At any rate, he couldn't be the one to complain to her.

"And don't you come back, neither!" George realized James was still talking, although most of what he was saying was an incomprehensible mutter. Only now and then did some line ring out clear. "Not, neither!" George heard James say as he slipped out the door.

George stayed in his old bed at the Garlands' that night, something he had continued to do on and off since moving in with his mother. He didn't always bother to tell her when he wasn't coming home—nowadays, unlike earlier times, she didn't always notice where he slept. George urgently wanted to talk to Chap, but he fell asleep before Chap came back from wherever he was. In the morning, George had to be at the docks by 6:00 a.m.

The next few times George saw him, James was more subdued. He even tried to be friendly toward George, an effort that in no way endeared him to George. George could sense something was off. Neither mentioned Chap or Lizzy.

These days George barely saw his mother, who was sewing from early morning to late evening, trying to pay back the money her clients had loaned her for her freedom purchase.

At the same time, George could not help but notice that James never worked. Surely, his mother must see this, too? George could not understand his mother at all. What had she needed to be married for? It was as if she had spoiled freedom with marriage. To George, Lizzy's marriage looked like just another form of slavery—slavery by choice.

One night, George was sitting in the kitchen at the Garlands' with Aggy, when she mentioned that she hadn't seen Chap for a few hours. "Sometimes I wonder if he has a sweetheart," she said. "I wish he did," she added, shaking her head. "He's pined after his poor wife for so long."

"I'm going to sleep at home tonight," George said.

"That's okay, honey," Aggy said. "You head on home and tell your mother 'hello' for me. But don't say a word to that stepfather of yours," she added. Aggy had not taken to James either.

George simply could not stop thinking about Chap and his mother. Whatever they were doing, neither of them wanted him or James to know about it. George decided that he would try to find out that night. His plan was to wait outside his mother's house until he saw Chap, then confront him.

It was a hot, muggy evening, and George was having trouble staying awake as he hid himself in a shadowy corner across the street from his mother's house. The sound of horses' hooves echoed in the distance. Most of the windows in the houses on the street were dark, as everyone seemed to be in bed. It was so quiet that he felt he could almost hear the wooden docks and boats groaning in the sluggish river.

After what seemed like hours of waiting, George saw Chap approaching his mother's house. But to George's surprise, Chap was not alone. A shorter figure was huddled against Chap's side, the short legs working frantically to keep up with Chap's longer stride. His head and shoulders were hidden beneath a floppy hat and plaid shawl. Then, George saw the front door to his mother's house open, and a woman emerged from the darkened doorway. George recognized his mother instantly. She met Chap and the other figure, and the three quickly circled the side of the house, vanishing from George's view. At that, George crept out from his hiding space, dashed across the street, and followed the three into the back. He arrived just in time to see them disappear into a cellar door that apparently opened into the ground.

George approached the cellar door. He pulled at the handle. The door gave way more readily than he'd expected, leading to a flight of stone stairs descending into the earth. Closing the door quietly behind him, he slowly made his way down the stairs. It was pitch dark, so he felt his way along the wall, to the bottom of the stairs, where he stood still, trying to catch his breath and orient himself. Off to his right he heard whispering. Following the voices, he rounded a corner and came upon Chap and his mother. Seated on the ground, between them, was the third figure George had seen. He had taken off his hat and shawl, and George could see his face. He could not believe his eyes. It was William!

Chapter 10

Making Plans

George stood amazed at the sight of his friend. How could it be? Everyone had heard that William was up north with his mother, Nancy, and his brother, John. George himself had seen William on his last night in St. Louis, when he had delivered the bundle containing the papers and clothing the three needed to escape. If William was in St. Louis, something must have gone terribly wrong.

George stood as still as a post; he did not know whether to reveal himself or to slip away unseen. But it was too late to decide, because wheeling around for an instant, his mother saw him.

"Georgie!" she whispered loudly. "Thank God it's you! I thought it was . . . I don't know who!"

George stepped forward into the small circle. At the sight of him, William gave a broad smile but said nothing. He looked tired, but he was clearly pleased to see George, who smiled back at his friend. If William wasn't in the North, at least he was safe, George thought.

"Shhh," Chap said. "We'll explain later." Then, turning to William, he said, "We're going to leave you here tonight, at least. You'll be fine. I'll come later with more food, water. Then, you'll see. You won't be here long. We're making plans to get you away, finally. Come on, George," Chap said, putting his hand on George's shoulder. "We have to go."

"Don't you worry, honey," Lizzy said to William. "We'll be back for you before you know it." She gave him a kiss on his forehead. George felt a pang of grief. He rarely saw his mother so tender these days, rarely felt her kiss on his forehead.

Outside the cellar, Chap went back to the Garlands' and George went into the house with his mother. He wanted to talk to her about what he'd seen. Everything that had happened—her new husband and new home, William's reappearance, even their new freedom—made George feel adrift in the world. Hugh Jr., the Garlands' oldest son, had once taunted George because he had no father and no last name by telling him he was "nobody's boy." "And nobody wants you," Hugh Jr. had added, as a flourish. Now James Keckly's words came back to George. He didn't know his mother, after all. She hardly treated him like a son.

James was snoring loudly in the back room, stretched out diagonally across the bed, when Lizzy and George came into the front room. They sat down at the table that served as a kitchen and parlor table. Lizzy lit the small lamp on the table, and it cast a small ring of light on the old, scratched wood. She began to explain.

"Nancy and the boys got to the river the night they were supposed to escape. But Mr. Lynch and Dr. Farrar had men down there watching. They had been told to look out for a mother and two boys, and it was just too dangerous to try to have them all escape, so Chap brought them back to Dr. Berry's church. Nancy wanted William and John to go on without her, but it made no sense. What were they supposed to do once they got up north, two young boys like that? They'd be kidnapped, or get into some kind of trouble. I talked to Nancy—mother to mother—and convinced her that it was better for her to go ahead with the younger one and find a place to live, and some work, then have William sent up to her. We could take care of William down here for her. She agreed, but you could see it near broke her heart to go without William, and I don't think she believed she'd ever see him again." George wanted to know where William had been hidden. "In the church basement, in attics, and now in our cellar," his mother said, quickly. "Even some white folks were willing to hide him." George immediately thought of the sounds he'd heard in the Garland attic when Louis was sick. Would the Garlands have known, he wondered. "There are some good white folks," his mother continued.

"But someone must have talked, and it's too dangerous to keep him here. We've got to get him out, soon."

George listened to his mother without taking his eyes off her face. How could all of this have been going on without his knowledge? How could his mother have done what she did? She had always been adamant about not participating in anything outright illegal because she was afraid of ruining her prospects for freedom. It was just the same now that she was free. She was firm in her desire to be, as she put it, "an upstanding citizen"—no different, and certainly no worse, than the white people she worked for. She was determined to rise in the world, determined to see her son rise, and because of this her reputation was everything. George was not surprised to see Chap involved, but his mother—that was another matter. It thrilled George to see this side of his mother, a side he never knew existed.

"What about the letters from New York?" George asked. "I thought they were from Nancy."

"They were," Lizzy responded. "But I wrote them for Nancy before she left and gave them to someone who carried them to New York to mail from there. She's not in New York, but she's not in St. Louis, either."

George didn't ask where Nancy was hiding, because it was clear his mother wasn't willing to tell him. Instead, he began thinking about what he could do to help William escape. Since the time he had chosen to hide from Mr. Garland instead of asking him to help William, George had felt he needed to redeem himself in his friend's eyes. He needed to show William he was willing to help, whatever the risk. The desire to do something was stronger than ever.

James began stirring in the next room, and Lizzy, putting her finger to her lips to indicate their conversation was over, stood up and went into the back, closing the door separating the rooms behind her. She left George at the table, where he sat a good long while, thinking.

Early the next morning, before going to work at the docks, George went to the Garlands' to speak to Chap. He found Chap collecting wood for the Garland fireplaces, a job George used to do when he was their slave.

"I have a plan for how William can escape," George began.

Chap put down the bundle of wood he'd been holding as George continued speaking. "I can pretend to be a white boy traveling with his slave. We can take the ferry to Bloody Island, to the train depot. We won't get caught. I can read and write and pass as a white boy. I know I can do it."

Chap listened respectfully to George, whose idea of passing himself off as white, Chap knew, was not out of the question. It might even work. George had been brought up among white people and could easily mimic their mannerisms and speech. George's idea attracted Chap's attention for another reason, as well. Chap had wondered how George felt about being white-skinned, or when and how George would take deliberate advantage of his appearance. Other slaves resented George's skin, but not Chap. He was glad to see George making use of his color as a weapon against oppression. Indeed, he liked the irony of George using his white skin against the white slaveholder. It really was the only benefit to a slave who happened to be light-skinned.

But first, they needed to have Lizzy's approval, which, to George's surprise, she gave without hesitation.

George himself told William, who was still hiding in the cellar, about the plan. "Do you think it really will work?" William asked. He was eager to get out of the damp, dark basement, but as usual, he looked to his friend for confidence. "Of course," George told William, wanting to sound firm and sure. "My mother will help us with clothes. All we need to do is say as little as possible. I'll pretend to be shy or sickly. My mother says we'll be left alone." William promised to be a good "slave" to George, who promised to be a good "master." It was a grim joke, and both boys felt it.

According to Chap, there was little time to waste. William's master and Mr. Lynch had been tipped off by somebody—Lizzy thought it was a slave woman in the home of one of the white women who had briefly hidden William in her attic—and had put out another flyer seeking Nancy and her sons' capture. Whatever plan they carried out, the real identities of both boys would need to be completely erased and new identities created. In her flowing handwriting, as fine as her mistress's, Lizzy wrote a letter supposedly to "Mr. Alexander Hobbs," inviting him to visit relatives in New York, signed "Aunt Mary." George wrote a pass for William, who could not write, stating that the slave boy, Edward, was traveling with his master to New York and back. The clothing was left up entirely to Lizzy, who kept a trunk full of material and clothes that she used for runaways; from this, she pulled a brown jacket and pants and a clean linen shirt for George and green cotton pants and a blue shirt for William.

Over the course of the few days that preparations for William's escape were being made, it became clear to George that his mother distrusted her new husband, and that all of the work they were doing had to be done without James's knowledge. The fact that his mother did not confide in James actually made George happy, even if it was probably a source of sorrow for her. She had waited so long to let herself marry and had married with such high hopes, George knew.

In the meantime, Chap was trying to find out which of the ferryboat captains had reputations for sympathy toward fugitives, just in case the boys needed help. He learned that there was a certain Captain Gregory who was expected to be on board the next Friday, and who was known to have turned a blind eye to runaways. Not all ferryboat captains would be so easy. It was Monday, but they decided to wait for Captain Gregory to be on duty. They also wanted to send word to some friends to meet the boys on the opposite shore to direct them to a safe house, where they could stay until the next stage of their journey was prepared.

But then, on the Wednesday night two days before the planned escape, Dr. Farrar, Anne Garland's son-in-law and John's owner, called on Anne to ask if she'd heard anything about Nancy. He had evidently thought nothing of speaking in front of Aggy, who was sewing in a corner of the parlor. Anne had heard nothing about the runaways, but then Dr. Farrar turned to look at Aggy as he asked, "Where is Lizzy living these days?" When Dr. Farrar left, Anne asked Aggy what she knew about Nancy and the boys, and Aggy told her what she believed—that they were up north somewhere. "Safe, I hope," Aggy added, under her breath.

Yet as soon as she could, Aggy told Chap about Dr. Farrar, and when Chap heard that Dr. Farrar was asking about the slaves, and that he had specifically asked where Lizzy lived, he told Lizzy that the boys had to cross the river that very night. They could not afford to wait any longer. They'd have to take their chances once in Illinois that their disguises would protect them from observation.

"Take care," Lizzy said to William when the time came for the boys to go. She gave him another tender kiss on his head. Then she turned to George. There were tears in her eyes as she looked her son over. "Don't come back if you can't or don't want to," she whispered in his ear, so that only he could hear her. "I will follow you." She hugged him tightly. Chap was hardly less sad at their parting. He did not expect George to return.

George had thought he'd be excited and happy to be leaving. But what he felt at that moment was deeply depressed. He didn't know if he'd ever see his mother or Chap again.

Chapter 11

Crossing the River

George and William walked quickly down to the north levee without speaking to each other. When they came to the ferry crossing, they fell into the jumble of people and livestock waiting to board to cross to Bloody Island, across the river in Illinois.

A tall man in an old coat and a beaver top hat stood in front of them, carrying a worn carpet bag with one hand and a walking stick. To calm himself, George concentrated on counting the creases in the back of the man's shiny, well-worn coat. William put down the bag he was carrying for his "master," but snatched it back up when he noticed the brown puddles of tobacco juice on the dock. Behind them, cows and horses, switching their tails, waited with apparent infinite patience.

George had tucked his lucky blue shirt inside the bag, along with the book of Burns poetry he had borrowed from the Garland library. Chap had packed the boys' passes and train tickets. Lizzy put in some money for emergencies and apples and biscuits for the boys to eat.

Once on board, the boys settled themselves on the flat wooden deck, trying as best they could to sit away from the rest of the passengers. No one spoke to them, which relieved George. He didn't want to respond to questions or make conversation with any stranger.

George kept his eyes turned on St. Louis and his thoughts on what his life had been as the ferry steamed away from the wharf. Nothing could make him wish to return to slavery, but he had to admit there were parts of his childhood he already missed, mostly the comfort and companionship of other slaves, like Chap. Since becoming free, he had felt slightly awkward around Chap, although he tried not to show it, and Chap gave no indication that he felt a change. It occurred to George that to be a former slave was its own category. He wasn't sure what it meant to be free. He was afraid that he'd always at heart be a slave.

When George was a small boy in Virginia, he used to feel like the friend of some of the white children who lived near the Garland plantation and played games with the black slave children who were owned by their parents and neighbors. But George's light skin made him the target of teasing, which only became worse as the children grew older. One white boy, a fat, pug-faced child whose skin was even a shade darker than George's, and who was disliked by everyone because he was a bully, once pushed George down in the dirt and told him that what he needed was "to get black," like his "nigger mother." None of the white boys and girls who knew George and saw him tumble into the dirt did anything to help him. They stopped briefly, wide eyed, then turned back to their play.

"Why, if it isn't Louis Kirkland!" George started at the sound of the name. Before him stood a large, red-faced man with a big cigar hanging perilously from the side of his mouth. He seemed to recognize George and to be speaking to him. "Running away again, I see." At this, William shot George a terrified glance. George tried frantically to think of a response. The only logical thing to say seemed to be "no," so that's what George said.

"Not like last time—it's been a couple of years, hasn't it? You've grown," the man said. He was evidently waiting for George to speak.

"Yes, sir. I mean, no, sir. I'm taking the train east to see my aunt."

"Your mother's sister?" the man inquired.

"Yes. My mother's older sister. My mother was going to go with me, but she's doing poorly, so she decided to have me go alone. My aunt has no children," George added.

"Your mother's sick?" the man asked. He removed his cigar from his mouth and began squinting at George, then at William, as if he were looking for something. The look of the man made George nervous. He couldn't remember who this man was, or why he was calling him Louis Kirkland. But it was making him sweat to be having this conversation without knowing what was going on.

Slowly, the man's face relaxed. "That's okay, sonny," he said, soothingly. "I understand. And this is . . . ?" he asked, looking at William.

"George, my slave," George answered. For the life of him, he couldn't remember what William's name was supposed to be. Fortunately, William, acting like he was deaf and dumb, said nothing. Instead, he gave the man a big grin.

"Which way are you heading?" the man asked.

George did not want to answer, for fear the man would be going the same way. But he said, "To Ohio."

"I'm heading to Kentucky," the man said, "so we won't be able to travel together. But good luck to you, sonny. And I hope your mother recovers real soon." He gave George another meaningful look, which George did not know how to interpret.

The man returned the cigar to his mouth, nodded once, and walked off a little distance. George stared after the retreating figure. Who was he? George vaguely remembered telling someone his name was Louis Kirkland, but he couldn't think of the time and place. What did the man mean by saying he was running away?

"Who was that?" William asked in a whisper.

"I don't know," George said.

"Well, he thought he knew you. I hope he leaves us alone," William said.

"Me, too," George answered.

Chapter 12

Saving a Friend

*T*he ferry docked, and all the passengers disembarked. George and William hurried off, William still carrying the bag with its precious contents. They followed the flow of passengers to the train depot. The man with the cigar had disappeared; so had the tall man in the tall hat.

The train was scheduled to leave in twenty minutes, so the boys had no time to take notice of their surroundings. Absorbed in the task of being inconspicuous, which is often a sure way to make oneself conspicuous, the two barely glanced around before boarding the waiting train. George settled himself in the first-class car, where white people rode, while William went to the car reserved for black people. The train gave off several puffs of steam, the whistle blew, and soon it began chugging away.

They had barely left the station when George saw the man with the cigar seated a few rows behind him. In fact, George smelled his cigar before looking around. He turned back instantly, hoping the man had not seen him. He was calmly puffing on his cigar and staring contemplatively out the window. George was horrified. What was he doing here? Wasn't he supposed to be on another train? It was then that George knew that the man must be a slave hunter hired to track down runaways, and that he somehow deduced that at least one of the boys was a fugitive trying to escape. If they were caught, George would certainly be charged with stealing and be jailed, while William's fate would be much, much worse.

George felt trapped. To reach the car carrying William, he would have to walk right past the man. He could get off at the next stop, but that would mean abandoning William without money, food, or papers. Before separating, William had handed George their bag, leaving William empty-handed. George decided that no matter what, he would not leave William to fend for himself. He couldn't live with himself were he to do that.

Gradually, George realized that the smell of cigar smoke was no longer behind him, but right above him. The smell of the smoke hovering over him reminded him of the first time he saw this man—on the steamboat where he'd hidden himself about three years before.

Could he pretend not to see him? George tucked his hands beneath his knees so that they would not shake. He stared straight ahead, as if nothing could budge him from his scrutiny of the empty seat facing him. The man slipped into the seat and, leaning forward, spoke in barely a whisper.

"You can trust me," the man began. "I won't say anything to anyone. My name is Elijah Moses, and I work for the Ohio Vigilance Committee. I can help you escape this time."

"I don't know what you mean. I am not running away. William is my slave."

Something in the man's eyes flickered in a knowing, final way, as if a latch had just shut decisively.

"The last time I met you, you were hiding on a steamer. I remembered you, because it's not every day you find a boy hiding behind a barrel. You said you lived with your aunt because your mother had died. I don't know why I remembered that, but I did. I suppose it's because I've always wondered if I'd prevented you from making your escape. I didn't want to take a chance, because I was helping someone else, and didn't want to put him at risk. He was hiding on board, too."

George did not know whether to trust this Elijah Moses or not. The vigilance committees that helped runaways were legendary among the slaves he knew. Anyone who devoted his or her life to helping slaves was a hero among the slaves.

"Today you told me your mother was alive and that you were going to visit your aunt," Elijah went on. "Of course, that made me suspicious. Just now you told me your 'slave's' name was William. Ten minutes ago it was George. Which is it? Anyway, I can help him, too."

For the first time, George examined Elijah Moses closely. He had coal black eyes and thick, coarse black hair, a wide mouth, and a generous nose. It dawned on George that this man could be like him—part black, part white. He told Elijah part of the truth—the part that mattered—that only William was running away, but that he was free. He did not tell him about his mother or Chap's role, and Elijah was discreet enough not to ask. George had learned that the people who worked to free slaves generally asked few questions and were satisfied with few details.

As the train approached the Illinois town of Alton, George was explaining to William the change in plan. William would travel on with Elijah, who had persuaded George that his familiarity with the railroad and his friends in the cities and towns along the route to New York made him the better guide and companion for William. Once again, George's idea of rescuing William went awry, but he could not say no to what was so obviously the surer plan.

Seated in the railroad car reserved for black people, George told William about Elijah. George's presence in the car attracted notice from some of the other passengers, but most ignored this white boy in their midst. George told William about the first time he'd met Elijah, and he confessed that the reason he'd run away was his fear of Mr. Garland's reaction to his losing his papers. "I knew he'd whip me, or find someone to do it," George said.

"I forgot to tell you," William exclaimed. "I found those papers in the street and brought them to that other lawyer for you."

"You found them? Why didn't you tell me?"

"I guess I just forgot. I meant to. But I forgot."

After all this time, George finally understood why Mr. Garland hadn't said a word to him about the lost papers. He hadn't known the papers had ever been lost. George realized that instead of him saving William, William had saved him.

At Alton, William and Elijah continued on the train north, while George bought a return ticket and waited for the return train to St. Louis. In the end, he knew he wasn't ready to leave the world he knew as home. His mother had told him he could stay in the North, on free soil, if he wanted to, and he had begun his journey sure that that was what he would do. It was strange, even frightening, to discover he wanted to return to the South—to being just George among folks who had known him as a slave. He didn't know what to make of himself. And his mother, what would she think? Or Chap? It seemed almost crazy to turn back. But that is what he did.

Epilogue

George remained in St. Louis with his mother and James Keckly until 1860, when Lizzy Keckly decided to move back east, without her husband, to seek her fortune. In the end, George was right to have distrusted his stepfather, who turned out to have lied about being free—he was actually a slave—besides being a deadbeat and a drunk, which they already knew. George, of course, was not sorry to see him fall from grace.

As for himself, George went up to Ohio to enroll as a student at Wilberforce University, a new school founded by the Methodist Episcopal Church to educate the free black sons of aspiring African Americans. Many of George's classmates were, like him, the mixed-race offspring of Southern plantation holders, and George finally laid claim to the name Kirkland, his planter father's name, and became known as George Kirkland.

By the spring of 1861, Lizzy Keckly was settled in Washington, D.C., where she established herself as a high-class dressmaker. George received a letter from his mother telling him about her new job: dressmaker to Mary Lincoln, the wife of the new president, Abraham Lincoln. George was not surprised. Ever since moving to Washington, his mother had talked about going to work for the women of the White House, and it had been George's experience with Lizzy that what she wanted she often got.

But while his mother's star was rising, the nation was plunging into crisis, as Southern state after Southern state seceded from the Union. Finally, in April, the crisis came to a head, shots were exchanged between the North and South at the federal garrison at Fort Sumter in South Carolina, and thousands of men marched off to war. White men, that is. Black men were not allowed to enlist in the Union Army when the Civil War broke out.

Sitting in a classroom studying history and philosophy while other men suffered to save the Union struck George Kirkland, by then a young man, as obscene. It seemed to him that this war was about all of the battles he had fought, or wanted to fight, since he could remember, battles against slavery and bigotry. For George, the Civil War was a personal war in more ways than one. Not only was it a fight for the rights of his family and his people, but the very idea of a civil war, of a body divided against itself, seemed to him to

Black soldiers on sentry duty.
Wood engraving, 1863. MHS Library.

mimic his own internal struggle about his color and identity. George knew that his white father would never have considered George his son, and had probably given George as much thought as he gave to an ant he might crush with his foot. It made George angry with himself that he still wanted recognition from this man, some acknowledgment that he was somebody's son. Why wasn't it enough to know that his mother loved him, in spite of his father and the circumstances of his birth?

When the war broke out, George felt more than anything that he needed to join the Union fight against the Confederate South. He returned to Missouri and, passing as a white man named George W. D. Kirkland, signed up as a soldier with the First Missouri Volunteers.

He was killed in his first fight, on August 10, 1861, in the terrible battle of Wilson's Creek in southwest Missouri, falling alongside the 2,600 men who were killed or wounded or went missing that day. His mother wept when she received the letter telling her about her son's death.

Timeline

February 1818	Lizzy Hobbs is born in Virginia
1820	Missouri enters the Union as a slave state in the Missouri Compromise
1839	George Hobbs is born to Lizzy
1846	Dred and Harriet Scott first sue for their freedom
1850	Fugitive Slave Law enacted
November 1855	Lizzy buys her and George's freedom
1857	U.S. Supreme Court rules that Dred Scott is and will remain a slave
November 1860	Abraham Lincoln is elected president
December 1860	South Carolina secedes
February 1861	Confederate States of America is created
April 1861	Fort Sumter is attacked by Confederate forces, beginning the Civil War

August 1861	George Hobbs is killed in the Battle of Wilson's Creek
September 1862	Battle of Antietam
January 1863	Emancipation Proclamation frees all slaves in rebel states
July 1863	Battle of Gettysburg
September 1864	General William T. Sherman captures Atlanta
November 1864	Abraham Lincoln is re-elected
January 1865	Congress approves the Thirteenth Amendment, abolishing slavery
April 9, 1865	General Robert E. Lee surrenders the Confederacy at Appomattox Courthouse
April 14, 1865	President Lincoln is assassinated
December 1865	Thirteenth Amendment is ratified by the states, abolishing slavery

Glossary

Dred Scott Case

In 1846, Dred and Harriet Scott, two St. Louis slaves owned by Dr. John Emerson, sued his widow for their freedom. Their lawsuit was based on the claim that they were free because they had lived on free soil with Dr. Emerson during the years he was stationed at military forts in Illinois and the Iowa territory. Hugh Garland was one of Mrs. Emerson's lawyers while the case was being decided in Missouri courts. In 1854, the Missouri circuit court ruled against the Scotts, and their lawyers decided to appeal the decision before the United States Supreme Court. In March 1857, the Supreme Court issued its ruling: Dred Scott was, and had always been, a slave. The Court also ruled that no black person could be a U.S. citizen, which meant that Dred Scott could not sue anyone in the first place. It was an important decision and increased the already growing tensions between the North and South.

Fugitive Slave Law

As part of the Compromise of 1850, a package of laws was enacted by Congress to enable California to enter the Union as a free state without upsetting the balance of power in Congress between Northern and Southern states. The Fugitive Slave Law required that runaway slaves who had escaped to the North (where slavery was outlawed) be returned to their owners. The Fugitive Slave Law of 1850 was not a new law, but rather a strengthening of an original fugitive slave provision written into the Constitution.

The Missouri Compromise

In 1819, when Missouri applied for statehood, a battle erupted in Congress over whether Missouri would be admitted into the Union as a slave state (where slavery was legal) or a free state (where slavery was illegal). Maine also asked to be allowed to join the Union, and this allowed Congressmen to reach a compromise in 1820. Missouri would enter as a slave state, while Maine would become a free state. In addition, slavery would be banned above the latitude 36°30'. The Compromise worked until the Kansas-Nebraska Act of 1855, which turned back the Missouri Compromise and allowed slavery to spread into the Kansas territory, west of Missouri. The conflict between North and South grew ever more intense as slavery spread west.

For Further Reading

Clinton, Catherine. *Scholastic Encyclopedia of the Civil War.* New York: Scholastic Reference, 1999.

Collier, Christopher, and James Lincoln Collier. *Slavery and the Coming of the Civil War: 1831–1861.* New York: Benchmark Books, 1998.

Edwards, Judith. *Abolitionists and Slave Resistance: Breaking the Chains of Slavery.* Springfield, NJ: Enslow, 2004.

Fleischner, Jennifer. *The Dred Scott Case: Testing the Right to Live Free.* Brookfield, CT: Millbrook Press, 1997.

Herda, D. J. *The Dred Scott Case: Slavery and Citizenship.* Springfield, NJ: Enslow, 1994.

Horton, James Oliver, and Horton, Lois E. *Slavery and the Making of America*. New York: Oxford University Press, 2005.

January, Brendan. *The Dred Scott Decision*. New York: Children's Press, 1998.

Lukes, Bonnie. *The Dred Scott Decision*. San Diego: Lucent Books, 1997.

Meadows, James. *Slavery: The Struggle for Freedom*. Chanhassen, MN: The Child's World, 2001.

Stanchak, John. *Civil War*. Dorling Kindersley Eyewitness Books. New York: Dorling Kindersley Publishing, 2000.

About the Author

Jennifer Fleischner is professor and chair of the English Department at Adelphi University in New York. She is the author of *Mrs. Lincoln and Mrs. Keckly: The Remarkable Story of the Friendship Between a First Lady and a Former Slave; The Dred Scott Case: Testing the Right to Live Free; I Was Born a Slave: The Story of Harriet Jacobs;* and *Mastering Slavery: Memory, Family, and Identity in Women's Slave Narratives.*